Who
the Tuskegee Airmen?

by Sherri L. Smith

illustrated by Jake Murray

Penguin Workshop
An Imprint of Penguin Random House

In honor of the Tuskegee Airmen on land
and in the air, to my brother, Derek,
and for every child who dreams of flight—SLS

For all those who weren't afraid to fly in the face
of adversity and injustice—JM

PENGUIN WORKSHOP
Penguin Young Readers Group
An Imprint of Penguin Random House LLC

Library of Congress Cataloging-in-Publication Data is available.

ISBN 9780399541940 (paperback)   10 9 8 7 6 5 4 3 2 1
ISBN 9781524786748 (library binding)   10 9 8 7 6 5 4 3 2 1

Contents

Who Were the Tuskegee Airmen?

January 20, 1945

The plane was not going to make it back to the airfield in Italy. US Airman Larry Fleischer shivered inside the B-24 bomber as it limped through the skies.

World War II had been raging for more than five years. In late 1941, the United States had joined with England, Canada, and other countries to defeat Nazi Germany and its allies.

B-24s played a major role in winning the war. Fleischer's plane, however, had been hit while dropping bombs on a Nazi air base in Austria. Two of the engines were out. The bombing doors in the belly of the plane had jammed open. The wind was roaring in at sixty degrees below zero. Fleischer had already lost a boot trying to unstick the doors.

Now, he was afraid he might lose his foot to frostbite. The plane needed to land soon. But where?

Down below, the Italian coast was fast approaching. Fleischer and the rest of the crew scouted for a safe landing area. It was the copilot who found their best hope. He spotted an airfield, but it was one that didn't show up on any of their charts.

"We really were expecting it to be a German field because why wouldn't it be on one of our maps?" Fleischer recalled. If that were true, the pilot and crew would be taken as prisoners. But there was no other choice.

The pilot carefully brought the plane in for a landing and saw that this was no German base. The runway was lined with American planes! Splashes of crimson paint marked these P-51 Mustangs as Red Tails. These fighter planes were famous for protecting American bombers in enemy skies.

The Red Tails had saved Fleischer and his crew on more than one bombing mission. As another crewman put it, "They were our lifesavers."

Fleischer and his crew were so relieved! They went out to greet the approaching soldiers, eager to finally meet the Red Tails face-to-face instead of in the air. What they saw was the surprise of their lives.

"These are all black guys!" Fleischer remembered thinking. "It was a complete shock!"

Why was it so surprising to see black pilots in 1945? Fleischer was a white guy from New York. His entire crew of ten men was white. The only black people Fleischer had ever seen in the army were cooks and waiters. Until now.

The Red Tails weren't just any combat pilots.

They were the famous Tuskegee (say: tus-KEE-gee) Airmen. They were the first airplane pilots of color ever in the US military. (*Military* means the armed forces of a nation.) But to Fleischer and his all-white crew, their existence was "more secret than the atom bomb!"

CHAPTER 1
Two Americas

By the end of 1939, World War II had broken out in Europe. The United States was not involved in the fighting yet. But the military wanted to be prepared, just in case. So the army had started the Civilian Pilot Training Program (CPTP) at many colleges and universities. (Civilians are people who are not in the armed forces.) The CPTP

was created to teach young Americans how to fly planes. If the country joined the war overseas, there would be more pilots ready for battle.

But not everyone could join the CPTP. It was for white people only.

A 1925 military report said that black men were not as smart or as brave as white men. The belief was that black people couldn't learn how to fly airplanes. But that was completely wrong!

Black people had been flying since 1917. An African American pilot named Eugene Bullard joined the French air force and fought against Germany in World War I. He won several medals for his bravery.

Eugene Bullard

Bessie Coleman

In 1920, a southern woman named Bessie Coleman went to France to learn how to fly. She became the first African American female pilot in 1921. Coleman returned to the United States, where she gave lectures and flew in air shows across the country. She wanted to raise enough money to start a flying school for African Americans. Unfortunately, in 1926 she was killed in a tragic airplane accident before that dream was achieved. Three years later, the Bessie Coleman Aero Club was founded in Los Angeles in her honor.

Jim Crow Laws

In the first half of the twentieth century, black people were segregated—kept apart—from white people in all sorts of ways. Especially in the southern states, black people could not live in the same neighborhoods as white people, eat in the same restaurants, or go to the same schools. There were signs in shop windows that said "For Whites Only,"

and even separate water fountains. The rules were known as Jim Crow laws.

These laws carried over to the military. Black soldiers lived in separate barracks from white soldiers and ate in separate mess halls. White officers could command black soldiers, but black officers were not allowed to command white soldiers. Black people were treated as second-class citizens *and* soldiers.

The name Jim Crow came from a silly, clumsy character in music shows of the early to mid-1800s. Jim Crow was supposed to be a black man but was always played by a white actor in black makeup. The character was meant to poke fun at and insult black people. In 1964, Jim Crow laws ended when the Civil Rights Act was passed by Congress.

In May 1939, two black men named Chauncey Spencer and Dale White flew an old airplane from Chicago to Washington, DC. They wanted to encourage other black people to become pilots.

Dale White   Chauncey Spencer

In Washington, they met with a senator named Harry S. Truman. (Truman would become president of the United States in 1945.) Truman saw the rickety old airplane the men had flown.

He said, "If you guys had the guts to fly that thing from Chicago, I've got the guts enough to do all I can to help you."

Harry S. Truman was true to his word. Later that year, Congress approved six Civilian Pilot Training Programs for black people. The most famous of these programs was at Tuskegee Institute in Alabama.

Harry S. Truman

Coffey School of Aviation

Willa Brown   Cornelius Coffey

The Coffey School of Aviation opened in 1938 in Chicago, Illinois, to teach black people how to fly. (Some of its graduates later became Tuskegee Airmen.)

Cornelius Coffey took his first flight when he was about thirteen. A barnstorming pilot came to town. Barnstormers were stunt pilots. The white pilot asked Coffey to board the plane so he could have some fun at the black child's expense. On the ride, the pilot threw the plane into spins, rolls, and a nosedive. He did his best to scare Coffey. But Coffey loved every minute of it. The pilot was impressed.

"He told me I should think about flying," Coffey told a reporter. However, he had trouble finding a flight school that would teach black people. So he and his friend John Robinson built their own airplane using a motorcycle engine and taught themselves.

Willa Brown knew Coffey and Robinson. She, too, was bitten by the flying bug. Four years later, she and Coffey opened a pilot training school where he "always put one white and one girl in every class of ten students. I wanted to prove to our government that whites and blacks, boys and girls, could be trained together."

CHAPTER 2
Taking Flight

Tuskegee Institute was a famous black college founded by Booker T. Washington in 1881 in the town of Tuskegee, Alabama. Unfortunately, the nearest airport was forty miles away. There was a lot of work to do before a CPTP program could be up and running.

The school rented a field to build its own airport. The first class had twenty students—eighteen men and two women. The students had to mow the field and create a runway. They built a hangar. (A hangar is a building where airplanes are kept.) It had room for three small airplanes called Piper Cubs. The students also built their own classroom.

Tuskegee Institute

Tuskegee Institute began in 1881 after a white politician, Senator W. F. Foster, asked a former slave how he could get African Americans to vote for him. The former slave, Lewis Adams, suggested starting a school for black people like him. So Senator Foster convinced the state of Alabama to establish the Tuskegee Normal and Industrial Institute. But who would run it? A teacher named Booker T. Washington, who had once been a slave himself.

Booker T. Washington

Washington served as teacher and president of the school from 1881 until his death in 1915. The Institute started out in a one-room shack with only thirty students. By 1915, the Tuskegee Institute had over fifteen hundred students and had become a leading school in the country. The Civilian Pilot Training Program at Tuskegee trained an estimated four hundred students. After the start of World War II, almost one thousand army pilots were trained as part of the Tuskegee Airmen program.

Today, the Institute is known as Tuskegee University and has over three thousand students.

The first part of learning to fly is called ground school. In ground school, students learn how to check the weather and how to read maps. They also learn the different parts of an airplane and how each one works.

Chief Pilot Charles Alfred Anderson was in charge of the first group of students. Anderson was one of the first African Americans to ever hold a pilot's license. Everyone called him "Chief." His students made national news when the entire class passed the written test for

Charles Alfred Anderson

ground school. No other class in the area—black *or* white—had passed everyone.

Soon, the school needed a bigger airfield and newer planes. Help came from a surprising source—the First Lady of the United States.

Eleanor Roosevelt was the wife of President Franklin Delano Roosevelt. She had her own weekly radio show and a newspaper column.

Eleanor Roosevelt

She traveled the country to meet with struggling Americans.

Eleanor Roosevelt loved flying! She had been friends with the famous female pilot Amelia Earhart. The First Lady was very interested in the Civilian Pilot Training Program. She thought women and African Americans should learn to fly, too.

Amelia Earhart

In March 1941, Eleanor Roosevelt stopped at Tuskegee's airfield. She wrote in a column about her trip that the training was "in full swing. . . . These boys are good pilots. I had the fun of going up in one of the tiny training planes with the head instructor, and seeing this interesting countryside from the air."

That instructor was Chief Charles Anderson. A picture of "Chief" and the First Lady smiling from the cockpit of his plane made newspapers across the country. That photo went a long way

toward showing white people that black people could indeed fly. Through Eleanor Roosevelt, a charitable fund lent $175,000 for a bigger airfield at Tuskegee. It was called Moton Field, after the second president of Tuskegee Institute, Robert Moton.

CHAPTER 3
We Need More Men!

In the fall of 1939, Adolf Hitler's Nazi army marched into Poland and seized it. That made Great Britain and France declare war against Germany.

Why didn't the United States of America immediately help to stop Hitler? The country was still suffering from the Great Depression, with millions of people out of work. There  were also some Americans who believed the United States should stay out of a conflict being fought so far away.

Then, on December 7, 1941, the Japanese

bombed the American naval base at Pearl Harbor in Hawaii. (The Japanese were allies—on the same side—with the Germans.)

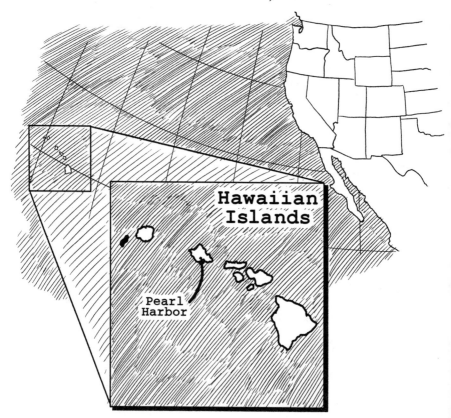

A day after the attack, the United States joined the war against the Axis powers—Germany, Italy, and Japan.

Franklin D. Roosevelt

In 1941, the United States military had only about 1.5 million soldiers. Now the army needed nearly six times that number. Even if every able man between the ages of eighteen and forty-five joined the fight, it still would not be enough. For the first time in US history, the country would call upon women and minorities for help as never before.

JOIN US in a VICTORY JOB

APPLY AT YOUR NEAREST NATIONAL SERVICE OFFICE

In World War II, many battles were fought in the air. So the United States needed pilots. Lots of them. Black people wanted to join the Army Air Force. But the US military was still not convinced of their ability. It did not want to mix black pilots with white pilots. And the army still claimed that black people did not have "the right stuff" to fly in a war. Black people insisted they were just as capable as anyone else. For them, the war was a chance for a "double victory." A double victory meant they wanted to stop the Axis powers overseas *and* help put an end to racism at home.

Even before the United States entered the war, a black CPTP student named Yancey Williams filed a lawsuit against the army. A lawsuit is a complaint that must be settled in court. Williams's lawsuit said the army had to prove that black men could not fly. But the success of the CPTP program at Tuskegee and other black institutions was clear proof that black people *could* fly.

On January 16, 1941, the army agreed to form an all-black squadron. A squadron is a group of pilots, instructors, mechanics, and other support staff. So Williams dropped his lawsuit.

A new military airfield was built not far from Moton Field. The men would train at Moton and the new Tuskegee Army Air Field. Williams would go on to become one of 992 pilots to graduate

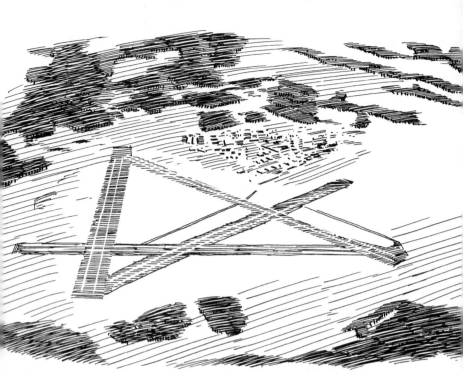

Tuskegee Army Air Field

from the Tuskegee Army Air Field program. It was known as the "Tuskegee Experiment" because the army did not think it would succeed. It would be up to the newly trained black pilots to prove the military wrong!

CHAPTER 4
The First Class

On July 19, 1941, the Tuskegee Civilian Pilot Training Program became a military training school instead. There were thirteen cadets in the first class. A cadet is an officer in training. The men came from all across the country—from Texas, Pennsylvania, Connecticut, New York, and South Carolina.

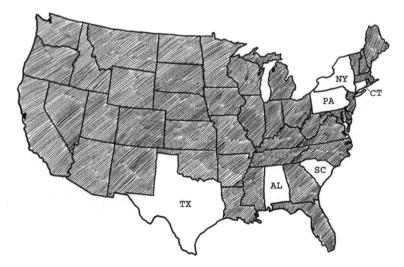

Lemuel Custis

Only two of the new cadets didn't already know how to fly. One was Lemuel Custis, the first black police officer in the city of Hartford, Connecticut. The other, Capt. Benjamin O. Davis Jr., had graduated from West Point. West Point trains its students to be army officers. During his years at West Point, Davis was the only black cadet. The school had refused to teach him to fly. Now, however, the army needed a black officer to command the new black squadron. (Davis was one of only two black officers in the entire military at the time— the other was his father, an army general.)

Benjamin O. Davis Jr.

Still, some people tried to keep Davis out of the Tuskegee program. A doctor said he failed his medical tests. A second test proved that the doctor had been lying. Davis was allowed to take part in the Tuskegee Experiment.

The town of Tuskegee was too small to even have a train station. The new arrivals were dropped off at a small station in nearby Chehaw. "Chee-haw!" the conductor cried.

Benjamin O. Davis Jr. (1912–2002)

Benjamin O. Davis Jr. had a lot to live up to. His father was the first African American general in the US Army. At the age of twenty, Davis Jr. entered West Point Military Academy where he was the only African American cadet in the entire school. His white classmates decided to "silence" him to show he was unwanted. That meant no one spoke to him outside of class. They would not eat at the same table with him. No one would room with him in a dormitory.

"This cruel treatment was designed to make me buckle, but I refused to buckle in any way," Davis wrote in a book about his experience. "First, I did not mention my troubles in letters to my mother and father. Second, I made my mind up that I would continue to hold my head high."

He went to New York City for New Year's Eve and met a young lady named Agatha Scott. She began to visit him at West Point. "Her visits never lasted long, but when she left I always felt as if my batteries had been recharged."

The "silencing" did not work. In June 1936, Davis became the first black man to graduate from West Point in the twentieth century. Eight days later, he married Agatha Scott. Davis went on to command the Tuskegee Airmen. He became the first African American general in the US Air Force.

There was not much to see. Cotton fields and pine trees stretched out beneath summer rains and humid heat. One soldier stepped off the train and into mud "around a quarter foot deep." But it wasn't just the weather that was a challenge.

Davis had lived in Tuskegee as a kid and knew the way black people were treated in the South. However, being in Alabama was a new experience for most of the other men. "A lot of the Tuskegee Airmen from New York and other places . . . were completely afraid," one airman who had gone to college in the South recalled. "Get on the streetcar, you go to the back, automatically. This is something that I just took for granted as the way of doing things," he said in an interview. But he didn't like it. "I lived to be part of the fantastic system that helped to change it."

When the first cadets arrived in Tuskegee, the air base was still being built. The black cadets had to sleep in an old bathhouse on the campus. The bathhouse had once contained an indoor swimming pool. A floor had been built over the pool. Bunk beds were arranged across the floor in two rows. Gear was stored in footlockers set at either end of the beds. After primary training, the cadets would move to Tuskegee Army Air Field. There, they would sleep in tents until the new barracks were completed.

The airfield was segregated. White soldiers and instructors at the base ate in a dining hall with black waiters and white tablecloths. The

Tuskegee cadets ate by themselves in a dining hall with dirt floors. On rainy days, the floors turned to deep Alabama mud. The men did not let it bother them. They were there to fly.

Tuskegee Base Commanders

At Tuskegee, the base commander was always a white officer. Base commander Col. Frederick von Kimble believed in segregation on the base, and he refused to promote black officers. Black newspapers complained about von Kimble until he was forced out of Tuskegee. Fortunately, his replacement, Cdr. Noel Parrish, had faith in the black cadets. "In fact, Parrish fought hard to see that the group was able to stay intact and to make sure we were treated fairly . . . if he had been hostile and racist, he could have made it really rough on us," Airman Roscoe Brown recalled. "They called it the Tuskegee Experiment because they expected it to fail, but Parrish helped it succeed."

Noel Parrish

CHAPTER 5
The Military Way

There were three stages in learning to fly the military way. Primary training, basic training, and advanced training. Each stage took about nine weeks. The first class of cadets began primary training in July 1941. If everything went well, the men would graduate the following March.

Primary training began at Moton Field. It included ground school and actual flying. The first planes the men flew were Stearman PT-17s. *PT* stands for "primary trainer." These were biplanes.

Biplanes are airplanes with two sets of wings stacked one above the other. The instructor sat in the back of the cockpit and flew. The student sat in front with his own set of controls. The instructor communicated through a speaking tube that connected to the student's headphones. The instructors would show the men what to do, and the cadets would copy them. They learned  how to take off, land, and handle emergencies in the air. Cadets made their first solo flights after about six hours of lessons.

Because Benjamin O. Davis Jr. and one other cadet, Lemuel Custis, had no flying experience, they had to learn all the basics that the others already knew. "I was consumed with making it,"

Custis said in an interview. "Next to my wife, flying has been the greatest love of my life."

Davis also recalled his flight training as a complete joy. "It was summer in Alabama, and flying over the green trees, the streams, and the orderly plots of brown farmland below was more exhilarating than anything I could have imagined."

Successful cadets moved on to basic training. In basic, they flew BT-13s. Cadets learned how to do loops, rolls, and steep climbing turns called chandelles. These sudden sharp movements might save their lives when faced with gunfire from enemy airplanes.

The men also learned how to fly at night. During the day, a pilot can see the sky and the ground. He can look for familiar objects to help him find his way. But at night, he must depend on the instruments in the cockpit to guide him. Lights and dials on the dashboard told how high

the plane was flying and how much fuel was left. There was also a compass to help point out the right direction.

Part of learning to fly at night was flying "under the hood." This meant a cadet would sit in a flight simulator. A flight simulator is a large box set up like a real cockpit. The instructor would cover the top of the box with a "hood." The cadet would have to learn to read the cockpit instruments in the dark.

Basic training was followed by advanced training. Here, the men were introduced to a whole new group of airplanes. Some flew fighter planes—AT-6s—while other pilots flew bombers—AT-10s and TB-25s. (*AT* stands for "advanced trainer." *TB* means "training bomber.") All the pilots also took much longer flights.

Beach AT-10 Wichita plane

Not every cadet made it to advanced training. Failing any part of flight school was called washing out. It meant not being allowed to fly. Cadets who washed out often became airplane mechanics and ground crew.

Tuskegee Airman Woodrow Crockett called training "the washing machine." "They washed out 75 percent of the cadets they took in . . . this was white boys," Crockett recalled. The Tuskegee

Airmen had a better record at 52 percent. Of the 2,053 cadets accepted into the program, 930 earned their wings.

The first class in the Tuskegee Experiment graduated in March 1942. Eight of the original thirteen cadets had washed out. Benjamin O. Davis Jr. and Lemuel Custis were among the five who made it. They were the very first black men to become Army Air Force pilots.

Front row: Lemuel Custis, Charles H. DeBow
Back row: Benjamin O. Davis Jr., George S. Roberts, Mac Ross

The Ground Crew

The title "Tuskegee Airman" didn't just apply to the pilot. Ground personnel who supported the pilots were also considered Tuskegee Airmen. This included flight instructors, mechanics, office workers, cooks, doctors, nurses, and janitors. The Tuskegee Experiment was one of the first military operations to include women as mechanics.

Fannie Gunn from Macon County, Alabama, was the first to sign on for the job. "We used to do a checkup on the airplanes before the cadets would fly," she said. She told one reporter, "I could fix anything in those days." This meant patching up bullet holes, repairing engines, and keeping the landing gear in working order. The Tuskegee women worked in Alabama throughout the war. They did such a good job that several received medals for their work.

Right away, the program started over again with a new group of black cadets. Soon there were thirty-three graduates, enough to form a squadron—the 99th Fighter Squadron (FS).

But if the Tuskegee Airmen expected to be sent overseas and see action right away, they were mistaken. Although the military was desperate for pilots, the Tuskegee graduates were left behind. The army still did not believe black pilots could succeed. So the graduates spent their days training and waiting for a chance to prove themselves.

CHAPTER 6
Red Tails!

By August 1942, five classes of pilots had graduated from the Tuskegee program. That was enough for two squadrons—the 99th and 100th FS.

By the spring of 1943, the United States had been fighting in the war for almost a year and a half. Finally, on April 15, 1943, new orders came. The 99th FS was sailing overseas to join the war! Benjamin O. Davis Jr., now a lieutenant colonel, was in charge of the squadron. The airmen were told to pack for cold weather and were put on a train to New York City.

Where were they being sent? That was a secret. Some thought England. German forces had been bombing the country for years. The 99th FS could help England fight back.

On a foggy day, the squadron boarded a ship called the SS *Mariposa*. (*SS* stands for "steam ship.") It was carrying both black and white soldiers. The men of the 99th FS were surprised to learn they were the highest-ranking officers on the ship. Since he was a lieutenant colonel, during the voyage, Davis Jr. became the second black man in command of white soldiers in the US military. His father had been the first.

The *Mariposa* docked in Casablanca, Morocco, nine days later. Morocco is a country on the northwest coast of Africa. It's a land of deserts and high mountains. The country was run by the French government.

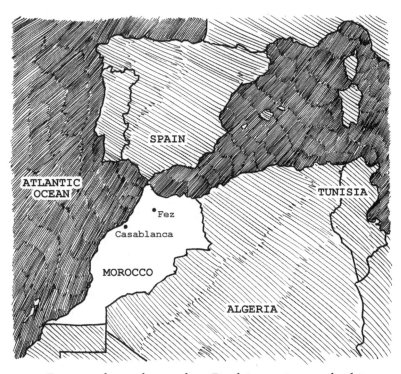

It was a hot, dusty day. Packing winter clothing had been a mistake. The men walked onto the crowded streets loaded down with heavy bags. There were no trucks to meet the 99th FS. They had to walk three miles carrying all their gear. In town, Airman Louis Purnell bought a bottle of Coca-Cola. It would be a prize for the first Tuskegee pilot to shoot down an enemy airplane.

The men boarded an old cattle train that took them to a base near the city of Fez. The base used to belong to the Germans. It was little more than a field at the foot of the great Atlas Mountains.

Airplane Art

One of the ways pilots identified their planes was with art painted on the front and sides of the aircraft. This was called nose art. Pilots would often paint a pretty woman or a fierce image on their planes. The famed Flying Tigers painted tigers or shark mouths on their airplanes. Lt. Col. Robert Friend had his wife painted on the nose of his P-51 Mustang. It showed a pretty lady dressed in yellow smiling brightly at the sky.

The former German base was littered with the wreckage of old planes. The men waited a week for their airplanes to arrive. The airplanes were called Curtiss P-40 Warhawks. The *P* stood for "pursuit." *Pursuit* means to chase. Pursuit airplanes were fighter planes.

The ground crew painted the tail of each P-40 plane a bright red. The splash of color would be easy to identify in the air. The Tuskegee pilots became known as the "Red Tails."

CHAPTER 7
Fighting in the Sky

In June 1943, the 99th FS moved to a new base in Tunisia. Tunisia is a country to the east of Morocco on the edge of the Mediterranean Sea. Here, the men were given their first combat sorties. *Combat* is another word for battle or attack. A sortie is any time a military plane takes flight.

One of the main jobs of the 99th FS was to protect other American airplanes on missions. Large planes called bombers carried explosives into enemy territory and dropped them there. Bombers were slow and heavy. They were easy targets for the enemy's smaller, faster fighter planes. That is why each bomber was protected by a group of its own fighter planes. The 99th

FS and other pilots would form a ring around the bomber. This was called an escort. Each pilot would keep a lookout for any trouble. The fighter planes would fight off enemy airplanes. They made sure the bomber reached its target safely.

Fighter planes battled enemy fighter planes in dogfights. Dogfights could be confusing. There might be more than one enemy plane on the attack. The enemy could be coming from all directions. They could even attack from above or below.

By the middle of the First World War, special mounts allowed pilots to put machine guns on their planes. A machine gun can fire many bullets quickly. A pilot only has to aim and pull the trigger. In World War II, machine guns became standard on every plane.

The Red Tails flew propeller-driven planes. A
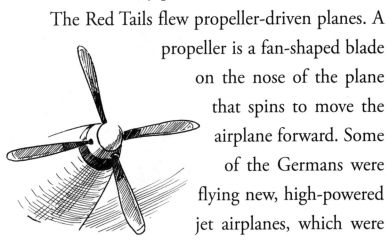
propeller is a fan-shaped blade on the nose of the plane that spins to move the airplane forward. Some of the Germans were flying new, high-powered jet airplanes, which were

much faster. However, the German jets were hard to turn. So American pilots in propeller planes learned to make tight turns in the air to get behind an enemy jet and fire at it. US fighter pilots also learned to point their airplanes toward the ground and swoop up at the last moment. This was called a dive bomb. An enemy jet would not be able to pull up as fast as a propeller plane. The jet would crash into the ground.

Dogfights in World War I

World War I (1914–1918) was the first war to use airplanes in battles. Before this war, planes did not have guns. No one had figured out how to mount a gun that a pilot could aim at passing planes without shooting through his own propeller or wings.

Instead, some pilots threw bricks or ropes at enemy planes. A brick could tear a wing. A rope could get tangled in the propeller that powered the plane. Most World War I pilots only had handheld pistols or rifles. It was possible to shoot an enemy pilot or an important part of the plane if you could fly close enough. These midair fights were the first dogfights.

On July 2, 1943, the 99th FS escorted sixteen B-25 bombers to attack a German airfield in Sicily. Sicily is an island off the southern tip of Italy. The mission was a success. As the planes turned to leave, bullets ripped the air. German fighters were

attacking from above! In an instant, two of the Red Tails were destroyed. Pilots Sherman White and James McCullin were the first men of the 99th FS to die in action.

There was chaos in the skies. The remaining Red Tails dodged and spun. They fired back at the enemy, protecting their bombers and fellow fighters.

Charles Hall swooped behind one of the enemy fighter planes. He fired a long burst from his guns. The German aircraft lurched, then fell from the sky. Hall was the first black pilot in the US military to "down"—destroy—an enemy airplane.

After the Red Tails shot down a second enemy plane, the Germans pulled back. The fight was over. The Red Tails escorted the bombers back to their home base. On the return trip, Hall did a victory roll in the air. Later, another airman drove fifteen miles into town to get a large block of ice.

Rules of Dogfighting

With these new planes came new ways of fighting. A British flying ace named Adolph "Sailor" Malan came up with ten rules for fighting other airplanes. The rules were often posted where other pilots could read them. Sailor Malan reportedly downed twenty-seven planes. It's no surprise his rules became popular with other fighter pilots!

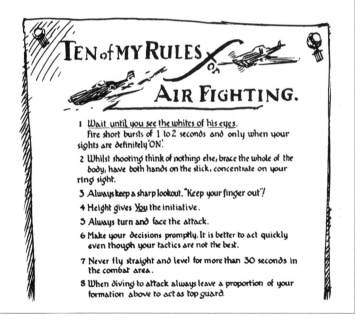

TEN of MY RULES for AIR FIGHTING.

1 Wait until you see the whites of his eyes.
Fire short bursts of 1 to 2 seconds and only when your sights are definitely 'ON'.

2 Whilst shooting think of nothing else, brace the whole of the body; have both hands on the stick, concentrate on your ring sight.

3 Always keep a sharp lookout. "Keep your finger out"!

4 Height gives You the initiative.

5 Always turn and face the attack.

6 Make your decisions promptly. It is better to act quickly even though your tactics are not the best.

7 Never fly straight and level for more than 30 seconds in the combat area.

8 When diving to attack always leave a proportion of your formation above to act as top guard.

The ice was used to chill the precious bottle of Coca-Cola. Hall enjoyed his prize in the shade of an olive tree. But it was a bittersweet victory. The Red Tails had lost two of their own.

CHAPTER 8
The Cost of War

Three hundred fifty-two Tuskegee pilots served overseas.

Sixty-eight died in combat or went missing in action. At least three Red Tails came close to ace pilot status. Thirty-one were held as prisoners of war.

On December 29, 1944, Lt. Robert Friend was in his plane, returning from a bombing escort mission in Germany. He had reached Italy and was flying over the mountains in bad weather when his plane started to have trouble. It was very hard to see.

Robert Friend

Aces

An ace is a pilot who has shot down five or more enemy airplanes. Pilots had to see the enemy plane fall from the sky for the "down" to count. Sometimes that was not possible in the heat of battle. Lee Archer, Edward Toppins, and Joseph Elsberry were each credited with four downs. Archer managed to shoot down three German airplanes in a single day of heavy combat. Earl R. Lane (100th FS), Charles V. Brantley, and Roscoe Brown each shot down a German jet. Jets could fly up to one hundred miles faster than the Red Tails' planes. That's some fast shooting!

Lee Archer

Friend knew he had to bail out, but he was afraid to do it over the ocean. "You end up in the water, you don't know which way is up," Friend later said. He also risked flying right into a mountain.

Friend couldn't wait any longer. He parachuted from his plane. He ended up tumbling down the slope of a mountain. He hurt his leg, but he was alive. He lay on the ground with his parachute tangled all around him. Suddenly a woman appeared with a knife! Friend soon found himself surrounded by local villagers. They all were holding weapons.

"Help! Help!" he cried out in Italian.

The people stopped. They looked at him closely. Was he an enemy German soldier? Not with that American accent and light brown skin!

"You're lucky you weren't speaking German," one of the men said.

"I'm lucky you can tell the difference!" Friend replied.

Friend was soon returned to his home base. He was given another plane, which he flew until the end of the war.

Other airmen were not so lucky. Alexander Jefferson was shot down over France. He had been on a mission with other fighters to destroy a radar station on the coast. Jefferson parachuted out of his airplane. The other pilots did not see him escape. His parents were told he was killed in action. In fact, Jefferson had landed in the trees above the very men who'd shot him down.

Jefferson was sent to a German POW camp.

POW is short for "prisoner of war." He was told he would have to share sleeping quarters with another American prisoner. He was surprised to be chosen by a white man from the South. He had "the deepest southern drawl imaginable," Jefferson recalled in an interview. The two men would have avoided each other back home. But the man was worried that other white prisoners might not really be "prisoners" at all. They could be German spies. When it came to guessing who was American, the white soldier could "trust a black man."

Soon another white American prisoner arrived in camp. The man had been a B-17 bomber crewman. He was very impressed when he found out that Jefferson was a Red Tail. "If the Red Tails had been with us, we'd have made it back home!" he said.

German Prisoners of War

Germans captured by American soldiers were sent to US prisoner-of-war camps. On some bases, the German prisoners were allowed to use facilities that the black American soldiers could not. That's how deep segregation ran in the US Army.

"German prisoners lived better than black servicemen," recalled Joseph P. Gomer, who never came in contact with white American soldiers. "We shared the sky with white pilots, but that's all we shared," he said.

The man's show of respect made other white soldiers treat Jefferson differently in the POW camp. They began to see him as an equal. There would be another nine months of war before these prisoners of war were set free. Until then, they were all Americans together.

CHAPTER 9
Target: Berlin!

The 99th FS left Tunisia for new bases in Italy. By October 13, 1943, enough cadets had graduated from Tuskegee to form more squadrons. The 100th, 301st, and 302nd Fighter Squadrons combined with the 99th as the 332nd Fighter Group (FG).

The Red Tails were earning a reputation as great fliers. They were dependable and stuck to their job. Not all pilots did. Some were more interested in becoming aces. They would chase after enemy fighters, hoping to get a "down." Doing this left their bombers dangerously unprotected. Lt. Col. Davis made sure his men did their duty. The Red Tails always stayed with their bombers.

They protected the bigger planes and earned a new nickname, the Red Tail Angels.

On June 25, 1944, the 332nd FG was returning to base. They spotted what appeared to be a German destroyer in the harbor at Trieste, Italy. A destroyer is a large warship capable of firing torpedoes underwater at other ships and shooting guns into the sky to bring down planes.

When the ship began to fire on them, the Red Tails moved in to attack. It was believed that destroyers were too big to be sunk by small fighter planes. But the Red Tails had been told lots of things weren't possible. They never let it stop them. The planes fired at the ship in a series of passes. Capt. Wendell Pruitt's bullets hit true. The big ship burst into flame. Lt. Gwynne Pierson followed behind with a spray of bullets. The ship exploded!

Later these two men were awarded the Distinguished Flying Cross for their "impossible" accomplishment.

Areas under German control, January 1945

The US Army Air Force was made of many moving parts. The 332nd FG was just one part of a larger group known as the Fifteenth Air Force. On March 24, 1945, the Fifteenth Air Force went on a mission to bomb Berlin, Germany. It would be the Red Tails' longest mission yet.

The city of Berlin is the capital of Germany. During the war, it was the heart of the Nazi government. Usually, bombing raids on Berlin were carried out by British pilots in planes coming from the west. This time, the Allies planned on surprising the Germans by sending *American* planes *north* from Italy instead. The Germans would not be expecting an attack from this direction.

The target was the Daimler-Benz tank assembly plant. The factory built armored tanks. It was extremely well-defended. Antiaircraft guns protected the plant from the ground. The airspace was patrolled by the best German pilots. These pilots would be flying new Me 262 jets. The new jets could fly up to one hundred miles per hour faster than the American Mustang P-51.

The Fifteenth Air Force knew about the faster German jets. So it gave its bombers more fighter plane escorts than ever before. The Red Tails

Me 262 jet

were determined to show their worth. They were assigned to escort the three lead bomber planes into Germany. They would protect the bombers above the factory. They were also expected to bring every single US bomber safely back to Italy.

One hundred sixty-nine B-17 bomber planes launched that day. Two hundred fifty-eight fighters joined them. The droning planes darkened the sky above the Daimler-Benz plant. The German antiaircraft guns around the plant began firing.

Many bomber planes missed their targets. The bombers couldn't aim well. They were too busy trying to avoid the enemy guns from below. The sky was soon filled with smoke.

Suddenly, three German jets attacked! The Red Tails and their fellow fighter pilots engaged in a series of vicious dogfights. They did their best to hold off the jets until the bombers had destroyed the factory.

Mission accomplished!

Eight German jets were shot down by the Mustang pilots. The 100th FS took out three of them. Never before had the Fifteenth Air Force shot down so many jets in a single day.

Sadly, fourteen American bombers were lost in the battle. The 332nd FG lost five of its fighter pilots as well. Ninety-three men of the Fifteenth Air Force never returned home from the raid.

The price was high, but the mission was still a success. The 332nd FG was awarded a

Distinguished Unit Citation for its good work. Their bombing run was the only one to hit the target dead-on. They had destroyed the Nazi factory and crippled the German army.

CHAPTER 10
Double Victory Denied

On May 8, 1945, the Nazis surrendered. The war in Europe was over. About two months later, the United States dropped the first atomic bombs on the Japanese cities of Hiroshima and Nagasaki. The Japanese army surrendered. World War II was over by mid-August.

The Red Tails were going home. They looked forward to being cheered, along with the rest of the returning soldiers.

In an interview with the *New York Times*, Lemuel Custis said, "When the Ninety-Ninth first went over the general impression was that it [the Tuskegee flight program] was an experiment. Now I think the record shows that it was a successful experiment." Black people could fly just as well as white people. They had "the right stuff."

Unfortunately, the Red Tails soon would see that even though they were war heroes, the United States had not changed its treatment of black soldiers.

Just that April, Red Tail officers had protested at Freeman Field in Indiana. They were angry because there were two separate clubs for officers. And they were not at all equal. The one for white officers had a game room with Ping-Pong, billiards, and tables for playing cards. It was next to the mess hall and even had its own fireplace. The club for black officers was a tired room with a couple of tables and a coal stove for heat.

Freeman Field Base

The black soldiers were arrested for protesting. The army eventually closed the white club rather than allow black people to use it.

There was a public outcry, however, over the arrests and the unfair situation. The army held a military trial called a court martial. It wanted to punish the soldiers for protesting. But the War Department had to admit that segregated clubs were unfair. The army made new rules that allowed for integration on military bases. But these rules were not always followed. The black soldiers were moved to another base where they received better treatment. Their action helped pave the slow road to equality in the military.

But when the Red Tails returned home from Europe, the men stepped off military ships onto American soil to be greeted by signs that said "Coloreds to the Left" and "Whites to the Right."

What kind of welcome was that? Had nothing changed at home? Didn't anyone know of the Tuskegee Airmen's brave service?

During the war, black newspapers had eagerly followed the missions of the Red Tails. Papers such as the *Chicago Defender* and the *Pittsburgh Courier* thought their accomplishments would result in a better life for and fairer treatment of black people in the United States. But white people didn't read black newspapers.

The Army Air Force even made a movie about the black pilots. *Wings for This Man* gave

a wonderful look at the heroism of the Tuskegee Airmen. But the film did not play in theaters with white audiences. The Red Tails were famous only in black communities.

After the war, commercial airlines would not hire a pilot of color. In the South, black war heroes still had to sit in the back of the bus. Even twenty years later, the Red Tails' deeds were mostly unknown. The daughter of a Tuskegee Airman told her college professor about her father's service. The professor said, "That can't be. There were no black pilots."

Some of the Red Tails were angry at being mistreated. They left the army. Some never flew again. Others continued in the military and as pilots. They kept working for the second part of their double victory—equality at home.

Then, in 1948, something big happened. Harry S. Truman was now president of the United States. Remember, it was Truman who had promised

Dale White and Chauncey Spencer to help blacks in aviation. In 1948, President Truman passed a law desegregating the United States Army. Black and white soldiers would now train and serve side by side. This was a huge victory for civil rights.

Still, it would take more years and more wars before the army and the other branches of the military were fully integrated. (*Integrated* is the opposite of segregated.) But integration did happen. In large part because of the brave service of the men of Tuskegee.

CHAPTER 11
Becoming Legends

So? What happened to the pilot training program at Tuskegee after the war?

In March 1945, right before the victory in Europe, the 302nd FS was deactivated. After the war, on October 19, 1945, the 332nd Fighter Group, including the 100th FS and the 301st FS, was also shut down. The Tuskegee Experiment was at an end. The military was not yet ready to call it a success. A recommendation was made for further "experiments" that would allow black and white soldiers to serve together. The 99th FS was assigned to a new flying group that included white squadrons.

Benjamin O. Davis Jr. went on to become a four-star general, the highest rank in the United

States Air Force. After the war, Lemuel Custis returned to Connecticut, where he went on to become the first African American chief of sales tax. Charles Hall, the first Tuskegee Airman to down an enemy plane, worked with the Federal Aviation Authority. POW Alexander Jefferson was freed from the prison camp near the end of the war. He returned to the United States and became an elementary school assistant principal as well as an air force reserve pilot. Chief Anderson trained pilots for years after the war and continued to fly until he was more than eighty years old!

Alexander Jefferson

Tuskegee Today

In June 1947, Tuskegee Army Air Force Base closed permanently. As for Moton Field, in 1972, the land was given to the city of Tuskegee, which still operates a small airport there today. The two original hangars are now part of the Tuskegee Airmen National Historic Site museum. The museum celebrates what is now known as the Tuskegee Experience—no longer an "experiment," but a success!

All told, the Red Tails flew 1,491 combat missions. They lost more than eighty pilots in action and in accidents. They earned ninety-six Distinguished Flying Crosses and over one thousand Air Medals for heroism in flight. Recent research shows that they may have received over forty-seven Purple Hearts for being wounded in combat. And they earned twenty-five Bronze Stars for heroism on the ground.

More than that, they created a legacy that continues to this day. The sky is for anyone who will brave it.

Timeline of the Tuskegee Airmen

1881 — The Tuskegee Institute opens in Tuskegee, Alabama

1917 — African American Eugene Bullard joins the French air force in World War I

1921 — Bessie Coleman becomes the first African American female pilot

1938 — The Coffey School of Aviation opens in Chicago, Illinois

1939 — Chauncey Spencer and Dale White fly to Washington, DC, and meet Senator Harry S. Truman

— World War II begins in Europe

— The Civilian Pilot Training Program begins at the Tuskegee Institute

1941 — Pearl Harbor is bombed and the United States enters World War II

— The "Tuskegee Experiment" begins with the first black pilots accepted into the US Army Air Force

1943 — The 99th Fighter Squadron and 100th Fighter Squadron are formed

— Charles Hall becomes the first black pilot to down an enemy plane

1945 — The 332nd FG successfully bombs the Daimler-Benz tank plant in Berlin, Germany

1947 — Tuskegee Army Air Field closes permanently

1948 — President Harry S. Truman signs the order to desegregate the US military

Timeline of the World

1882	Thomas Edison brings electric light to one square mile in New York City
1903	The Wright brothers' plane has its first successful flight at Kitty Hawk, North Carolina
1912	The RMS *Titanic* sinks on its maiden voyage
1915	Booker T. Washington, founder and first president of the Tuskegee Institute, dies
1917	The United States enters World War I
1920	Nineteenth Amendment gives women the right to vote
1927	Charles Lindbergh flies the first nonstop solo transatlantic flight
1931	The Empire State Building in Manhattan opens
1936	African American Jesse Owens wins four gold medals at the Summer Olympics in Berlin, Germany
1937	Famous female aviator Amelia Earhart disappears in her plane somewhere in the South Pacific
1939	World War II begins after Hitler's troops invade Poland
1945	World War II ends
	Harry S. Truman becomes president
1954	The Supreme Court bans segregated schools
1964	Civil Rights Act is passed
1965	Voting Rights Act is signed into law

Bibliography

*Books for young readers

*Brooks, Philip. *The Tuskegee Airmen: We the People*.
Minneapolis: Compass Point Books, 2005.

Caver, Joseph, Jerome Ennels, and Daniel Haulman. *The Tuskegee Airmen: An Illustrated History, 1939–1949*. Montgomery, AL: NewSouth Books, 2011.

Davis, Benjamin O., Jr. *Benjamin O. Davis, Jr: American: An Autobiography*. Washington, DC: Smithsonian Institution Press, 1991.

*Gubert, Betty Kaplan, Miriam Sawyer, and Caroline M. Fannin. *Distinguished African Americans in Aviation and Space Science*. Westport, CT: Oryx Press, 2002.

Moye, J. Todd. *Freedom Flyers: The Tuskegee Airmen of World War II*. New York: Oxford University Press, 2010.